THE DECEPTION ABOUT DEATH

THE FOURTH ANGEL'S PUBLISHING

The Devil's Deception About Death

Copyright © 2016 by The Fourth Angel's Publishing.

Design copright © by The Fourth Angel's Publishing,
PO Box 136637, Fort Worth, TX 76163.

Unless otherwise noted, Bible texts in this book are from the King James Version.

Printed in the USA.

978-0-9712-0976-3

Contents

MESSAGES FROM BEYOND 5

WHAT HAPPENS AT DEATH 11

LAZARUS, COME FORTH 18

"I SAY UNTO THEE, ARISE" 24

IMMORTALITY 28

THE THIEF ON THE CROSS 35

TWISTED TEXTS 45

The Devil's Deception About Death

MESSAGES FROM BEYOND

Where are our beloved dead? Where do people really go at death? Do they haunt houses? Are they reincarnated? Do they perhaps go to some place called limbo or purgatory? Could it be that they are simply floating around on a little pink cloud strumming a harp? Are they possibly in heaven or hell? That last one is not a very pleasant thought, is it? Yet all of these are prominent teachings in the world today. All religious groups (and even the non-religious) believe one or more of the above.

For example, some years ago Tanya Tucker claimed to have been visited by the spirit of Elvis Presley. The city fathers of Liberty, Missouri advertised for a psychic to conjure up the ghost of Jesse James. Some archeologists even claim that they are assisted in their discoveries by the spirits of ancestors.

The Devil's Deception About Death

While living in California I was amazed at an article which appeared in the local newspaper (The Saint Helena Star) with the heading The 89 Lives Of Marcy Calhoun. The article was about one of the local residents who claimed to have been reincarnated at least 89 times over the centuries. Her belief was that in the days of Amonhotep IV (ca 1375-1358 B.C.) she had worked as a servant girl in Pharaoh's palace. She was supposedly a witch twice in the past. She participated in the persecution of Christians in Rome. She had also lived in the south during the Civil War. She was burned alive in France and buried alive in Germany in past lives. She is deathly afraid of frogs because she was once sacrificed to a large reptile idol in China.

Anglican Bishop James A. Pike wrote of his communications with his dead son. Notice carefully the responses to the father's questions. "I'm working real hard at learning that being dead is really being more alive" declared the supposed spirit of the dead son.

> "Q. Have you by now heard anything about Jesus?
> "A. I haven't heard anything personally about Je-

sus. Nobody around me seems to talk about him. When we come over here we have a choice; to remain as we are, or to grow in our understanding. Some still seem to be church-minded and are waiting for a Judgment Day, but these seem to be the unenlightened ones. Others seem to be expanding their minds and self toward more eastern understandings." The Other Side, pp. 186, 187

"Q. Have you heard anything over there about Jesus, or a Jesus?
"A. I haven't met him. They talk about him - a mystic, a seer, yes, a seer. Oh, but Dad, they don't talk about him as a savior. As an example, you see? I would like to tell you Jesus is triumphant, you know? But it's not like that. Not a savior, that's the important thing - an example." The Other Side p. 324

Rosemary Brown gained notoriety when she composed 400 symphonies solely from the instructions given her by the spirits of such famous composers as Litz, Beethoven, Bach, Brahms, Chopin, and others.

Another spiritualist, Jane Roberts, noted for the Seth Letters and the biography of Jean Dixon has given these chilling accounts of her communications with the dead.

"All souls have one continuous existence through and infinite number of lives. God exists as the totality of all souls, living and dead, all matter, all energy. There is no heaven, hell, or purgatory, except of the soul's own making." The World Beyond "Your father says the most important story in the world for you to write is this: 'I live and we are in a world of activity and growth. We are not living in a vacuum - I am as vital and just as active now as when I was a boy.'" The Search for Truth, p. 27

"Fletcher said: He sends you his love. He doesn't remember about dying, and says he hasn't found anyone over here who does. There is no dying. All of a sudden you're free, that's all. Over here you have no ills. You're mature, but not old. He enjoyed his funeral very much. It was beautiful and simple, but he wasn't dead. He had merely gotten rid of a sick body." The Search for Truth, pp. 24, 25

Who are these spirits of spiritualism? The Bible gives a clear and distinct answer to this mystery. "They are the spirits of devils, working miracles" (Revelation 16:14). When we look at the first book of the Bible we discover the very first lie ever told on planet earth was "Ye shall not surely die" (Genesis 3:4) and that same lie is being perpetuated by spiritualists today.

"Spiritualism says that the dead know more than the living. 'And the serpent said unto the woman, ye shall not surely die.' Genesis 3:4. In this, as in many other Bible passages, the Devil told the truth and the Lord is in error." E. W. Sprague, Spiritualist.

Jesus declared: "Ye are of your father the devil, and the lusts of your father ye will do. He was a murderer from the beginning, and abode not in the truth, because there is no truth in him. When he speaketh a lie, he speaketh of his own: for he is a liar, and the father of it" (John 8:44). God says people die, but the spiritualists continue to promulgate the satanic lie that they do not die.

"The fundamental principle of spiritism is that human beings survive bodily death, and that occasionally, under conditions not yet fully understood, we can communicate with those who have gone before." J. Arthur Hill, Spiritism: History, Phenomena, and Doctrine, p. 25.

"There is no death in the graveyard" declared Sir Oliver Lodge. "I have frequent talks with the dead. I cannot doubt that people live after death for I frequently talk with them." Does a person really die? Are they able to communicate with the living? Should we attempt to talk with the dead through various mediums? The only infallible source of truth to these types of questions is found in the word of God.

"And when they shall say unto you, Seek unto them that have familiar spirits, and unto wizards that peep, and that mutter: should not a people seek unto their God? for the living to the dead? To the law and to the testimony: if they speak not according to this word, it is because there is no light in them" (Isaiah 8:19, 20). The living are not to attempt to communicate with the dead and to keep away from those who claim to have communication with the dead. These are the children of darkness and "there is no light in them."

WHAT HAPPENS AT DEATH

Why is it that so many people believe things contrary to what God's word says? Could it be that so few people go to the Bible to find truth, but are content to unquestionably believe what someone else has told them? The Bible tells us clearly that when a person dies he or she never returns to their house again. "As the cloud is consumed and vanisheth away: so he that goeth down to the grave shall come up no more. He shall return no more to his house, neither shall his place know him any more" (Job 7:9, 10). If this is true how can it be that some have supposedly seen and even communicated with the dead? Who or what are these apparitions? In these types of encounters what the individual encounters are "the spirits of devils, working miracles" (Revelation 16:14).

We have been warned that in the last days, "some shall depart from the faith, giving heed to seducing spirits and doctrines of devils" (1 Timothy 4:1).

The Devil's Deception About Death

Remember, the first devilish doctrine ever taught on this earth was that man does not really die. Genesis 3:4-5. The Genesis account of creation is very vital in understanding this subject; for if we want to know where we are going we need first discover where we came from. Only God can give the answer to either of these two things. Ask man where we came from and his response is monkeys or some other lower life form. Ask man where we are going and he says we are evolving to ever higher plains and greater heights.

I am reminded of a story I once heard of a young boy walking through the cemetery when he came across a tombstone that read: "Stop my friend, as you pass by. As you are now, so once was I. As I am now, you soon shall be. So, prepare yourself to follow me." The boy contemplated that for a moment, then reaching in his pocket he pulled out a crayon and wrote on the tombstone: "To follow you I'm not content, until I know just where you went."

Some believe that at creation man was created with an immortal soul. However, this premise has two great flaws in it. First, man did not receive a soul, he "became a living soul." "And the LORD God formed man of the dust of the ground, and breathed into his nostrils the breath of life; and man became a living soul" (Genesis 2:7). Second, nowhere in the Bible is a soul said to be immortal. As a matter of fact the Bible teaches, "The soul that sinneth, it shall die" (Ezekiel 18:4). That which is immortal is not subject to death, it cannot die.

So then what happens when a person dies? What exactly does the word of God say? Centuries ago Job asked the questions "If a man die shall he live again?", and "man dieth, and wasteth away: yea, man giveth up the ghost, and where is he?" (Job 14:14, 10). The answer to this is far different from what many are being taught today. "So man lieth down, and riseth not: till the heavens be no more, they shall not awake, nor be raised out of their sleep" (Job 14:12). "His sons come to honour, and he knoweth it not; and they are brought low, but he perceiveth it not of them" (Job 14:21).

All people were from the dust and when they die they all return to the dust. "For that which befalleth the sons of men befalleth beasts; even one thing befalleth them: as the one dieth, so dieth the other; yea, they have all one breath; so that a man hath no preeminence above a beast: for all is vanity. All go unto one place; all are of the dust, and all turn to dust again" (Ecclesiastes 3:19, 20). Not only does the body return to dust, but also every man's spirit returns to God. "Then shall the dust return to the earth as it was: and the spirit shall return unto God who gave it" (Ecclesiastes 12:7). This refers to the wicked as well as the righteous.

Many are confused as to what the spirit is, but the spirit is nothing more than that which God breathed into Adam's nostrils when He created him from the dust. That is the breath of life. "All the while my breath is in me, and the spirit of God is in my nostrils" (Job 27:3). "Thou hidest thy face, they are troubled: thou takest away their breath, they die, and return to their dust" (Psalm 104:29). Can you see how it fits together? Dust plus spirit (or breath) equals a "living soul." Dust minus spirit equals a "dead soul." Death is simply creation in reverse. This is true of all God's creation. "And they went in unto Noah into the ark, two and two of all flesh, wherein is the breath of life." "And all flesh died that moved upon the earth, both of fowl, and of cattle, and of beast, and of every creeping thing that creepeth upon the earth, and every man: All in whose nostrils was the breath of life, of all that was in the dry land, died" (Genesis 7:15, 21, 22).

When God takes the breath of life (spirit) from man he dies and returns to dust, regardless of the type of person he was. In this state there is no knowledge, wisdom, hatred, envy, work, etc. "For the living know that they shall die: but the dead know not any thing, neither have they any more a reward; for the memory of them is forgotten. Also their love, and their hatred, and their envy, is now perished; neither have they any more a portion for ever in any thing that is done under the sun.

Whatsoever thy hand findeth to do, do it with thy might; for there is no work, nor device, nor knowledge, nor wisdom, in the grave, whither thou goest" (Ecclesiastes 9:5, 6, 10). At that point in time they know nothing and they do not come back. As the righteous Job declared: "When a few years are come, then I shall go the way whence I shall not return" (Job 16:22). This is especially interesting in light of the belief that the spirits haunting houses or other places are doing so because of love, hate, or envy. Do you see how contrary this is to the word of God that says that the dead cannot experience these emotions for they have no knowledge whatsoever? Even Hollywood bombards us with supposed "family" films as Ghost, Ghost Dad, Casper, Jack Frost, and a host of others that promote this great error.

In that very day their thoughts perish, they can no longer even praise the Lord. "Put not your trust in princes, nor in the son of man, in whom there is no help. His breath goeth forth, he returneth to his earth; in that very day his thoughts perish" (Psalm 146:3-4). "The dead praise not the LORD, neither any that go down into silence" (Psalm 115:17). "For in death there is no remembrance of thee: in the grave who shall give thee thanks?" (Psalm 6:5). "For the grave cannot praise thee, death can not celebrate thee: they that go down into the pit cannot hope for thy truth. The living, the living, he shall praise thee, as I do this day: the father to the children shall make known thy truth" (Isaiah

38:18, 19).

The Devil's Deception About Death

LAZARUS, COME FORTH

We have a tremendous illustration of what death is like in the story of the raising of Lazarus. "Now a certain man was sick, named Lazarus, of Bethany, the town of Mary and her sister Martha. (It was that Mary which anointed the Lord with ointment, and wiped his feet with her hair, whose brother Lazarus was sick.) Therefore his sisters sent unto him, saying, Lord, behold, he whom thou lovest is sick. When Jesus heard that, he said, This sickness is not unto death, but for the glory of God, that the Son of God might be glorified thereby. Now Jesus loved Martha, and her sister, and Lazarus. When he had heard therefore that he was sick, he abode two days still in the same place where he was" (John 11:1-6).

Notice that when Jesus heard that Lazarus was ill He stated that it would not result in death, but that He and the Father would be glorified by what was about to happen. He then remained where He was for another two days before leaving from Bethany. It had taken the messenger one day to reach Jesus, Jesus did not leave for two days, and it will take Jesus one day to travel to Bethany. When He arrives He is told that Lazarus has been dead for four days (John 11:17). Thus, Lazarus had died the very day the messenger had left and was already dead when he reached Jesus.

After two days Jesus says: "Our friend Lazarus sleepeth; but I go, that I may awake him out of sleep. Then said his disciples, Lord, if he sleep, he shall do well. Howbeit Jesus spake of his death: but they thought that he had spoken of taking of rest in sleep. Then said Jesus unto them plainly, Lazarus is dead" (John 11:11-14). It is interesting that what we call death God considers to be sleep. Even the disciples had trouble grasping this concept.

When Jesus reached the outskirts of Bethany the news spread quickly and as soon as Martha heard she went out to meet Jesus. "Then said Martha unto Jesus, Lord, if thou hadst been here, my brother had not died. But I know, that even now, whatsoever thou wilt ask of God, God will give it thee. Jesus saith unto her, Thy brother shall rise again. Martha saith unto him, I know that he shall rise again in the resurrection at the last day" (John 11:21-24).

Jesus assures Martha that her brother will live again, but notice Martha's response. "I know that he shall rise again in the resurrection at the last day." She knew that her brother was dead and not alive in some other place and that he would live again in the future. Then "Jesus said unto her, I am the resurrection, and the life: he that believeth in me, though he were dead, yet shall he live: And whosoever liveth and believeth in me shall never die. Believest thou this? She saith unto him, Yea, Lord: I believe that thou art the Christ, the Son of God, which should come into the world" (John 11:25-27). What glorious good news. Because of Jesus, those who have died believing in Him shall live again "in the resurrection at the last day." And those who are alive never really die, they simply sleep until He comes and awakens them.

Jesus now sends Martha to get her sister Mary and "when Mary was come where Jesus was, and saw him, she fell down at his feet, saying unto him, Lord, if thou hadst been here, my brother had not died" (John 11:32). Jesus was moved with compassion for the mourners; both for their sorrow and their unbelief and "he groaned in the spirit, and was troubled" (John 11:33).

"Jesus wept" (John 11:35). Not as some have believed because of Lazarus' death, for He knew He was about to raise him from the dead. It was the cold, critical, unbelief that brought Jesus to tears. "Some of them said, Could not this man, which opened the eyes of the blind, have caused that even this man should not have died?" (John 11:37). The record states: "some of them went their ways to the Pharisees, and told them what things Jesus had done. Then gathered the chief priests and the Pharisees a council, and said, What do we? for this man doeth many miracles" (John 11:46, 47). "Then from that day forth they took counsel together for to put him to death" (John 11:53).

Knowing all these things, "Jesus therefore again groaning in himself cometh to the grave. It was a cave, and a stone lay upon it. Jesus said, Take ye away the stone. Martha, the sister of him that was dead, saith unto him, Lord, by this time he stinketh: for he hath been dead four days. Jesus saith unto her, Said I not unto thee, that, if thou wouldest believe, thou shouldest see the glory of God?" (John 11:38-40).

"Then they took away the stone from the place where the dead was laid. And Jesus lifted up his eyes, and said, Father, I thank thee that thou hast heard me. And I knew that thou hearest me always: but because of the people which stand by I said it, that they may believe that thou hast sent me. And when he thus had spoken, he cried with a loud voice, Lazarus, come forth" (John 11:41-43).

It is a significant fact that Jesus did not say "Lazarus, come down;" for if he had died and gone to heaven (as so many believe happens at death) he would have surely gotten a dirty deal. Neither did Jesus say "Lazarus, come up," as if from a hell or some such place. Had that been the case he would have gotten one of the best deals ever given. Neither was the call "Lazarus come back," as to a disembodied spirit roaming aimlessly or inhabiting some other body or form of life. The command was simply "Lazarus, come forth." Come out of that grave where you have been laid, "come forth." The voice of the Son of God pierces the ears of the dead "And he that was dead came forth, bound hand and foot with graveclothes: and his face was bound about with a napkin. Jesus saith unto them, Loose him, and let him go."

What Lazarus experienced was only a sleep, a four-day nap if you will. This is the way God has repeatedly portrayed death throughout the Bible. "And when thy days be fulfilled, and thou shalt sleep with thy fathers" (2 Samuel 7:12). The psalmist put it this way. "Consider and hear me, O LORD my God: lighten mine eyes, lest I sleep the sleep of death" (Psalm 13:3).

"I SAY UNTO THEE, ARISE"

A couple of other encounters Jesus had with death may prove helpful in fully grasping the condition of one in death. It is early fall of A.D. 29 and Jesus and His disciples are journeying along a hot, dry, dusty trail from Capernaum to Nain. (Luke 7:11). As the group make their way along a steep, rocky path to the city of Nain, about a half mile before they reach the city they pass a rock hewn burial ground; still in use today. As they draw near the village a funeral procession is seen coming out of the gates of the city in route to that cemetery. With slow sad steps it proceeds toward the place of burial. The body of the dead is carried before the procession on an open bier. All about it are the mourners. The deceased was the only son of his mother, and she a widow.

The lonely mourner moved on blindly, weeping, not even aware of Jesus' presence. He comes close to her and says gently, "Weep not." He then touches the bier and the bearers stand still. The weeping ceases as the people gather closely about the bier. They are hoping against hope. One was present who had banished disease and vanquished demons; was death also subject to His power? Then the Son of God speaks. "Young man, I say unto thee, arise." That voice pierces the ears of the dead and he awakes. Soon that same voice will pierce the ears of all of the children of God who are now resting from their labors. "For the Lord Himself shall descend from heaven with a shout, with the voice of the archangel, and with the trump of God: and the dead in Christ shall rise first" (1 Thessalonians 4:16).

The story of Jairus' daughter, found in Mark 5:22-43, again reveals the condition of one who dies. As Jesus is making His way to the young girl a messenger comes with the message "Thy daughter is dead: why troublest thou the Master any further?" But "As soon as Jesus heard the word that was spoken, he saith unto the ruler of the synagogue, Be not afraid, only believe" (Mark 5:35, 36). "And he cometh to the house of the ruler of the synagogue, and seeth the tumult, and them that wept and wailed greatly. And when he was come in, he saith unto them, Why make ye this ado, and weep? the damsel is not dead, but sleepeth. And they laughed him to scorn" (Mark 5:38-40).

They began to mock and ridicule Jesus for saying the girl was only sleeping. After all they were professional mourners they ought to know whether a person is dead or not. "But when he had put them all out, he taketh the father and the mother of the damsel, and them that were with him, and entereth in where the damsel was lying. And he took the damsel by the hand, and said unto her, Talitha cumi; which is, being interpreted, Damsel, I say unto thee, arise. And straightway the damsel arose, and walked; for she was of the age of twelve years. And they were astonished with a great astonishment" (Mark 5:40- 42). Again, that voice pierced the ears of the dead and she awoke. When Jesus comes "all that are in the graves shall hear His voice, And shall come forth" (John 5:28-29). "Verily, verily, I say unto you, The hour is coming, when the dead shall hear the voice of the Son of God: and they that hear shall live" (John 5:25).

"I SAY UNTO THEE, ARISE"

The great reformer and founder of the Lutheran Church, Martin Luther, understood this concept well when he wrote: "We shall sleep until He comes and knocks on the little grave and says, Doctor Martin, get up! Then I shall rise in a moment, and be happy with Him forever." The Christian Hope, p. 37

Death is consistently (53 times) referred to as a sleep in the Scriptures. In unconsciousness there is no concept of time. Whether a day, month, year, or 1,000 years it will make no difference. When Jesus comes those who have died in Christ will be awakened from their sleep and it will be as if it had only been a moment.

The Devil's Deception About Death

IMMORTALITY

The Bible truth of death and the resurrection was already being corrupted at the time of the apostles. Therefore, the apostle Paul addressed the issue head-on. "Now if Christ be preached that he rose from the dead, how say some among you that there is no resurrection of the dead? But if there be no resurrection of the dead, then is Christ not risen: And if Christ be not risen, then is our preaching vain, and your faith is also vain. Yea, and we are found false witnesses of God; because we have testified of God that he raised up Christ: whom he raised not up, if so be that the dead rise not. For if the dead rise not, then is not Christ raised: And if Christ be not raised, your faith is vain; ye are yet in your sins. Then they also which are fallen asleep in Christ are perished" (1 Corinthians 15:12-18).

Paul emphatically states that if there is no resurrection of the dead then they are "perished." How can this be if the dead immediately soar to heaven upon death as is taught by so many today? There would not even be a need for a resurrection.

The apostle continues: "If in this life only we have hope in Christ, we are of all men most miserable. But now is Christ risen from the dead, and become the firstfruits of them that slept. For since by man came death, by man came also the resurrection of the dead. For as in Adam all die, even so in Christ shall all be made alive. But every man in his own order: Christ the firstfruits; afterward they that are Christ's at his coming" (1 Corinthians 15:12-23). Again Paul is explicit in his affirmation that the resurrection of the dead does not occur until the second coming of Christ and without this resurrection to life all would have perished.

When Jesus comes not only will the righteous dead be raised, but the righteous living shall be changed "in a moment, in the twinkling of an eye" and both groups shall rise up "to meet the Lord in the air: and so shall we ever be with the Lord" (1 Thessalonians 4:17).

"Behold, I show you a mystery; We shall not all sleep, but we shall all be changed, In a moment, in the twinkling of an eye, at the last trump: for the trumpet shall sound, and the dead shall be raised incorruptible, and we shall be changed. For this corruptible must put on incorruption, and this mortal must put on immortality. So when this corruptible shall have put on incorruption, and this mortal shall have put on immortality, then shall be brought to pass the saying that is written, Death is swallowed up in victory. O death, where is thy sting? O grave, where is thy victory?" (1 Corinthians 15:51-55).

It is imperative that we not be deceived by the devilish doctrine that man is by nature immortal. We are mortals (Job 4:17; Romans 6:12; Romans 8:11; 2 Corinthians 4:11) and there is not one reference in God's word about man having an immortal soul. The King James Bible uses the word soul 1,600 times, but never once is it in reference to immortality. As we have seen in the above passages from 1 Corinthians 15, immortality is something that the righteous receive at the second coming of Jesus. Until that day scripture is clear that it is "the King of kings, and Lord of lords; Who only hath immortality, dwelling in the light which no man can approach unto; whom no man hath seen, nor can see: to whom be honour and power everlasting. Amen" (1 Timothy 6:15, 16).

"The pagan doctrine of the immortality of the human soul crept into the back door of the church." William E Gladstone. The ancient Egyptians, Romans, Greeks, Babylonians, and all pagan religions have believed this great error; as do all Satanist cults today. The eastern forms of ancestor worship are based upon this false doctrine of the immortality of the soul. "Ancestor worship in most cases is simply the Spiritualism of the East which serves as the exponent of immortality." Contact With The Other World, p. 14.

The prophet, Isaiah, declares: "Thy dead men shall live, together with my dead body shall they arise. Awake and sing, ye that dwell in dust: for thy dew is as the dew of herbs, and the earth shall cast out the dead" (Isaiah 26:19). This is why David declared, "I shall be satisfied when I awake, with thy likeness" (Psalm 17:15). In speaking of David, Peter declared: "Men and brethren, let me freely speak unto you of the patriarch David, that he is both dead and buried, and his sepulchre is with us unto this day" and then in the clearest language possible states, "David is not ascended into the heavens" (Acts 2:29, 34).

According to Scripture God's people will rest in the grave until the plagues containing God's wrath (Revelation 15:1; 16:1) are over; and then He will call them forth. "O that thou wouldest hide me in the grave, that thou wouldest keep me secret, until thy wrath be past, that thou wouldest appoint me a set time, and remember me! If a man die, shall he live again? all the days of my appointed time will I wait, till my change come. Thou shalt call, and I will answer thee: thou wilt have a desire to the work of thine hands" (Job 14:13-15).

"But I would not have you to be ignorant, brethren, concerning them which are asleep, that ye sorrow not, even as others which have no hope. For if we believe that Jesus died and rose again, even so them also which sleep in Jesus will God bring with him. For this we say unto you by the word of the Lord, that we which are alive and remain unto the coming of the Lord shall not prevent [precede] them which are asleep. For the Lord himself shall descend from heaven with a shout, with the voice of the archangel, and with the trump of God: and the dead in Christ shall rise first: Then we which are alive and remain shall be caught up together with them in the clouds, to meet the Lord in the air: and so shall we ever be with the Lord. Wherefore comfort one another with these words" (1 Thessalonians 4:14-18).

The Devil's Deception About Death

THE THIEF ON THE CROSS

A question that invariably arises is: "What about the thief on the cross? Didn't he go to heaven with Jesus the day he died?" Many have rejected the Bible teaching about death because of a misplaced coma. The passage in question is where the thief "said unto Jesus, Lord, remember me when thou comest into thy kingdom. And Jesus said unto him, Verily I say unto thee, To day shalt thou be with me in paradise" (Luke 23:42, 43). Remember, the original manuscripts of the Bible did not have chapter, verse divisions, or even punctuation. All these were inserted by translators to enable us to better understand and more readily find Scripture. In the vast majority of cases these people did an excellent job. However, in some cases even the division of chapters have been somewhat off causing an abrupt end to the writer's thought, which is then picked up in the continuing chapter. The same is true with punctuation, which has changed from generation to generation. But none have caused as much problem as the comma of verse 43. If the comma belongs before the word "today" it would mean that the thief would be in paradise that day. However, if the comma belongs after the word "today" it would simply mean that the thief was being told that day he would have a place in paradise when Jesus returns. How then can we know biblically where the comma belongs?

The word of God has not left us in the dark concerning this issue and has given us several things to enable us to know with certainty what Jesus told the thief.

>1. The thief was not even asking for something immediate when he said "remember me when thou comest into thy kingdom." 2. Neither of the thieves probably died that day.

>Because the Jews did not want anyone on a cross on the Sabbath the soldiers broke the legs of the two thieves, but when they came to break the legs of Jesus they found He was already dead and "they brake not his legs." John 19:31-33.

3. Jesus, Himself, did not ascend to heaven the day of His crucifixion. Three days later on the resurrection morning Jesus told Mary "Touch me not; for I am not yet ascended to my Father: but go to my brethren, and say unto them, I ascend unto my Father, and your Father; and to my God, and your God" (John 20:17).

4. Unless Jesus said: "Verily I say unto you Today, you shall be with me in paradise" it casts disrepute upon the rest of the Bible, which unequivocally states the dead remain in the grave until Jesus returns and calls them forth. One passage of Scripture should never be used in contradiction to the fulness of Scripture.

5. It was this assurance that enabled the apostle Paul, while awaiting execution, to declare "I have fought a good fight, I have finished my course, I have kept the faith: Henceforth there is laid up for me a crown of righteousness, which the Lord, the righteous judge, shall give me at that day: and not to me only, but unto all them also that love his appearing" (2 Timothy 4:7, 8).

The Devil's Deception About Death

I once read an account of a dying father who summoned his children to his death bed - and being a Christian family he pulled each one close a said "goodnight my child, I'll see you in the morning." But to the younger son, the "black sheep" of the family, the father said "goodbye my son." Startled by this the boy pulled back in horror crying "Father, you told the others good night and me goodbye. Please Father, tell me goodnight also." To this the father, with great sobs and flowing tears could only respond "Son, you have chosen a path in life, that unless changed, will prevent us from ever being together again. I pray that you will change so that on that resurrection morning our goodbye will become good morning."

In the catacombs beneath Rome can still be seen the places of hiding for both Christians and pagans. These people lived, died and were buried beneath this ancient city. However, there is one striking difference between the burial places of these two groups of people. Where the pagans buried their dead are found such inscriptions as "good-bye for all eternity" or "good-bye forever;" whereas in the Christian area the inscriptions read "good-bye until we meet again" or "good-bye until the morning."

Yes, dear reader, our fondest hopes are often blighted here. Our loved ones are torn from us by death. But hope bears our spirits up. We are not parted forever, but we shall meet the loved ones who sleep in Jesus. "They shall come again from the land of the enemy" (Jeremiah 31:16). The Life-giver is coming. Myriads of holy angels will escort Him on His way. He bursts the bands of death - breaks the fetters of the tomb - and the precious captives come forth in health and immortal beauty.

Soon the Life-giver will call up His purchased possession in the first resurrection, and until that triumphant hour, when the last trumpet shall sound and the vast army shall come forth to eternal victory, every sleeping child of God shall be kept in safety and will be guarded as a precious jewel, who is known to God by name.

Horatio G. Spafford lost everything in the Chicago fire in 1871 and it appeared it could get no worse. His health became so bad that his physician told him he needed to get away for a while. So in 1873 he sent his wife an daughters on ahead to Europe while he finished up some business before following. The ship carrying his wife and four daughters sank and he received a wire from his wife stating "All lost. Only I remain." Immediately Mr. Spafford departed to Cardiff, Whales where the survivors had been taken. In route he asked the captain to point out the spot where his daughters perished. It was there where his daughters had been drawn down into the cold, numbing, waters of the Atlantic that he penned the words that have brought such hope and comfort to untold numbers of people.

> *When peace, like a river, attendeth my way, When sorrows like sea billows roll*
> *What ever my lot, Thou hast taught me to say, It is well, it is well with my soul.*
> *Though Satan should buffet, though trials should come, Let this blessed assurance control,*
> *That Christ has regarded my helpless estate, And hath shed His own blood for my soul.*
> *And, Lord, haste the day when my faith shall be sight, The clouds be rolled back as a scroll:*
> *The trump shall resound and the Lord shall descend, "Even so" it is well with my soul.*
> — *Horatio G. Spafford*

Even though his sorrow was as tremendous and all encompassing as the waves of the great deep which had taken his children from him, he, by faith, looked forward to the coming of Jesus and the fulfillment of the promise that "the sea gave up the dead which were in it; and death and the grave delivered up the dead which were in them" (Rev. 20:13).

Jesus does not like death. It was never a part of His divine plan. He does not like to see His children sad and hurting. Yet there are more graves than houses on this planet. Nearly a half century ago my grandfather died and when I visited that grave several weeks after the funeral I was shocked to see a tombstone containing not only my grandfather's name, but the name of my grandmother who was still living. When I inquired of my parents concerning this frightful oddity I was told that she knew she would die one day and it was just easier to do it this way. They were correct, for nearly 30 years later that grave that had been waiting with her name on it claimed my grandmother. That area of the cemetery that was just an open field back then is now full and that small family plot on the southeast corner today marks the resting of grandfather, grandmother, father, brother, sister, and son.

The Devil's Deception About Death

It was not until many years later that I learned that Jesus came to do away with tombstones, to do away with death. Death was never a part of His plan. In the beginning everything was "very good," but sin entered this world and the "wages of sin is death." Inasmuch as "all have sinned and come short of the glory of the glory of God" "Death is passed upon all men in that all have sinned." Yes, "The wages of sin is death" - BUT - "The gift of God is eternal life." "And this is life eternal, that they might know thee the only true God, and Jesus Christ, whom thou hast sent." (John 17:3)

The questions I want to leave you with are immense in their eternal implications. "Do you know the Lord Jesus Christ?" "Do you know Him intimately?" "Do you have a growing, on-going relationship with Him?" Not on again, off again. "Do you daily seek to know Him better?" Your eternal destiny could depend upon your response to these questions.

Many years ago I came across an old story about a couple of young boys who set out to discredit the wisdom of an old sage living on a nearby mountain.

Their scheme was to catch a bird and take it to the old man with the question "Is the bird alive, or is it dead?" If the man answered "alive" they would crush it and let it fall to the earth, but if he said "dead" they would release it a let it fly away. On the appointed day they took their bird and departed on their journey. Arriving at their destination they approached the elderly man with the question "Is the bird alive, or is it dead?" The aged man looked at them intently for a time and then responded "The answer to that, boys, is in your hands."

Jesus is soon going to return to this earth for His people. Will you be ready for that day? The answer is still in your hands. It is going to take place whether you are or not. It is a day we should be looking forward to. It is a great reunion day. What blessed hope is found in the soon coming of the Lord Jesus Christ.

"And I heard a great voice out of heaven saying, Behold, the tabernacle of God is with men, and he will dwell with them, and they shall be his people, and God himself shall be with them, and be their God. And God shall wipe away all tears from their eyes; and there shall be no more death, neither sorrow, nor crying, neither shall there be any more pain: for the former things are passed away" (Revelation 21:3, 4).

TWISTED TEXTS

Peter warned that the Scriptures contain "some things hard to be understood, which they that are unlearned and unstable wrest, as they do also the other scriptures, unto their own destruction" (2 Peter 3:16). Following are a few examples of this.

> *"Therefore we are always confident, knowing that, whilst we are at home in the body, we are absent from the Lord:.... We are confident, I say, and willing rather to be absent from the body, and to be present with the Lord."* – 2 Corinthians 5:6-8

Beginning with verse one, Paul contrasts the present mortal state of the Christian with the future immortal life in heaven. Notice the expressions he uses to contrast these two conditions:

Present Mortal State	Future Immortal State
earthly house	building of God
this tabernacle	house not made with hands
mortality	our house which is from heaven
in the body	absent from the body
absent from the Lord	present with the Lord

The Devil's Deception About Death

Paul refers to being clothed with "our house which is from heaven" (Verse 2) and that he longs "that mortality might be swallowed up of life" (Verse 4). The key to understanding what Paul is saying is found in the description of a third condition.

After stating his desire to be clothed with immortality, Paul declares that" being clothed we shall not be found naked" (Verse 3). He further proclaims in verse four: "Not for that we would be unclothed."

It is evident that the naked or unclothed state was neither mortality nor immortality, but rather death and the grave. It is evident throughout Paul's writings that he neither taught nor believed that one passed instantly from being clothed with this tabernacle into being clothed with our house from heaven. He knew and Scripture reveals that death and the grave came in between, and this he referred to as being unclothed and naked.

Elsewhere in Scripture Paul spelled out exactly when the change from mortality would take place. In 1 Corinthians 15:52,53, he wrote, "The trumpet shall sound ... and this mortal must put on immortality." That will be when Jesus comes.

TWISTED TEXTS

"For I am in a strait betwixt two, having a desire to depart, and to be with Christ; which is far better:"
—Philippians 1:23

The Apostle Paul is not saying in this text that he will go to be with Christ when he dies. He is, without question, using the word "depart" in reference to his death. However, the Word of God explicitly reveals that Paul did not believe his "departure" would mean immediate entrance into heaven at the time of his death as the following reveals. "The time of my departure is at hand. I have fought a good fight, I have finished my course, I have kept the faith: Henceforth there is laid up for me a crown of righteousness, which the Lord, the righteous judge, shall give me at that day; and not to me only, but unto all them also that love his appearing" (2 Timothy 4:6-8).

Since Paul obviously did not expect to get his eternal crown at his departure in death, when was it that he anticipated actually being with Christ? "For the Lord himself shall descend from heaven ... and so shall we ever be with the Lord." 1 Thessalonians 4:16,17. Can you see the absolute clarity of this? Paul's desire to depart and be with Christ involved the resurrection that would take place at the end of the world. Since the unconscious sleep of death is like a moment, Paul speaks of death and the coming of Christ as almost simultaneous. And so it will seem to those who depart and awake from death to see Jesus coming.

> *"And it came to pass, that the beggar died, and was carried by the angels into Abraham's bosom: the rich man also died, and was buried; And in hell he lift up his eyes, being in torments, and seeth Abraham afar off, and Lazarus in his bosom."*
> –Luke 16:22,23

Many attempt to make this story about the rich man and Lazarus literal. However, there are several reasons why this cannot possibly be correct:

1. This story is given in the heart of some of the best known parables in the Bible. Luke 12:16 - The Foolish Rich Man; Luke 13:6 -The Fig Tree; Luke 14:7 - Wedding Seating; Luke 14:16 - The Great Supper; Luke 15:3 - The

Lost Sheep; Luke 15:8 - The Lost Coin; Luke 15:11 - The Prodical Son; Luke 16:1 - The Unjust Steward; Luke 16:19 -The Rich Man and Lazarus; Luke 18:1 - The Unjust Judge; Luke 18:9 - The Pharisee and Publican;
Luke 19:11 - Faithful Stewardship; Luke 20:9 - Rebellious Servants; Luke 21:29 - Signs of the Times.

2. The beggar died and was taken by the angels to Abraham's bosom. (Apparently Abraham is in charge of heaven). No one believes that Abraham's literal bosom is the abode of the righteous dead. It is a figurative or parabolic expression. Incidentally, the angels will gather the saints, but according to Matthew 24:31, this will take place at the coming of Jesus, not at a person's death.

3. Heaven and hell were separated by an enormous gulf, and yet the persons in each could converse with each other, even though the gulf was vast it could not be crossed. There are probably few individuals in the world who believe that this will be literally true of the saved and the lost (Luke 16:26).

4. Receiving "good things" in this life merit's torment in hell, whereas receiving "evil things" can assure you of heaven (Luke 16:25).

5. The rich man was in hell with a body. He had eyes, a tongue, etc. (Luke 16:24). How did his body get into hellfire instead of into the grave? I know of no one who teaches that the bodies of the wicked go into hell as soon as they die. This story could not be literal.

6. The request for Lazarus to dip the tip of his finger in water and come through the flames to cool the rich man's tongue is obviously not literal. How much moisture would be left and how much relief would it give? The whole story is unrealistic and parabolic.

In this parable the rich man represented the Jews because only a Jew would pray to "father Abraham." The beggar symbolized the Gentiles, who were counted unworthy to receive the truth. In Matthew 15:27, the Canaanite woman acknowledged that her people were beggars at the table of the Jews.

Later Jesus would actually raise a man named Lazarus from the dead. (See John chapter 11). The major point of this entire parable is found in Luke 16:31: "If they hear not Moses and the prophets, (the Scriptures) neither will they be persuaded, though one rose from the dead." As Jesus warned in the parable, they didn't believe even when Lazarus was raised before them, but "from that day forth they took counsel together for to put him to death" and "consulted that they might put Lazarus also to death; Because that by reason of him many of the Jews went away, and believed on Jesus" (John 11:53; 12:10, 11).

The Devil's Deception About Death

I KNOW THAT MY REDEEMER LIVETH

I know that my Redeemer liveth, And on the earth again shall stand;

I know eternal life He giveth, That grace and power are in His hand.

I know His promise never faileth; The word He speaks, it cannot die;

The cruel death my flesh assaileth, Yet I shall see Him by and by.

I know my mansion He prepareth, That where He is there I may be;

O wondrous thought, for me He careth, And He at last will come for me.

I know, I know that Jesus liveth, And on the earth again shall stand;

I know, I know that life He giveth, That grace and power are in his hand.

Where are our beloved dead? Where do people really go at death? Do they haunt houses? Are they reincarnated? Do they perhaps go to some place called limbo or purgatory? Could it be that they are simply floating around on a little pink cloud strumming a harp? Are they possibly in heaven or hell? All of these are prominent teachings in the world today. Every religious group (and even the non-religious) believe one or more of the above.

Why is it that so many people believe such a conflicting array of thoughts concerning the same topic? Could it be that so few go to the Bible to find truth and are simply content to unquestionably accept what someone else has told them without individual investigation?

With no absolute standard of truth and error mankind is left to develop a wide variety of beliefs; based primarily upon tradition and superstition and governed solely by their presuppositions and personal preferences.

The Bible gives very clear and distinct answers to this mystery. The Genesis account of creation is very vital in understanding this subject; for if we want to know where we are going we need first discover where we came from. Only God can give the answer to either of these two things. Therefore, this book will trace what the Bible teaches from Genesis to Revelation exposing The Devil's Deception About Death.

PO Box 136637
Fort Worth, TX 76163
(817)919-7267
www.fourthangelpublications.com

THE FOURTH ANGEL'S
PUBLISHING

The millennium is a subject that has for years arrested the attention of people world wide. The word itself does not appear in the Bible, but comes from a compound of two Latin words "mille" and "annum," which means simply, "thousand years." This thousand-year period, called the millennium, is mentioned six times in the first seven verses of Revelation chapter twenty and refers to that period of time in which Satan is to be bound and perfect peace and happiness will reign in the universe.

There are many various theories regarding the millennium which have been based largely upon speculations and fictitious novels. Some have even claimed that the devil has already been bound and we are now in the millennium. To this insanity a minister once replied, "If the devil is bound, he must be tied with a rubber chain that stretches from Paris to Bombay and from Washington, D.C. to the Kremlin." All we need to do is look about us to see that the devil has never been more active than he is today. This is why the Word of God warns us, "Be sober, be vigilant; because your adversary the devil, as a roaring lion, walketh about, seeking whom he may devour" (1 Peter 5:8).

This book will reveal there is no reason for anyone to experience confusion or uncertainty in regard to the millennium, for the Bible speaks quite clearly and in much detail on this subject presenting most clear, concise, and concrete statements pertaining to this thousand-year period.

PO Box 136637
Fort Worth, TX 76163
(817)919-7267
www.fourthangelpublications.com

THE FOURTH ANGEL'S
PUBLISHING

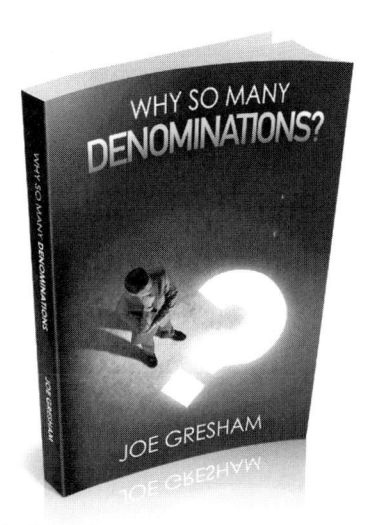

Have you ever wondered, if there's one God and one Bible, why there are so many different churches that dot the hillsides. The world has thousands upon thousands of church congregations and with this multitude of denominations people often wonder: "How can I find the truth? How can I know what truth is?"

There are over 220 denominations in the United States, comprising more than 320,000 Christian churches. You can start at the beginning of the alphabet and go to Assembly of God and then on to the Baptists, to Congregationalists, to Disciples of Christ, etc.. You can go through the alphabet and there will be a name for a church based on nearly every letter of the alphabet; all the way to Zionists. Every one of these churches claiming they have the truth.

Never will one of those churches hang a sign on its door that says: "Don't come in here, because you'll find error and not truth" or "We have the best mixture of truth and error available today?" With this collection of confusing concepts how can one discover truth?

The Bible clearly presents why there are so many different denominations and it helps us find our way through the maze of confusion. It helps intelligent, thinking, rational people to understand where these churches came from, and how to sort out truth from error. As one studies Bible prophecy they will understand what happened to the early Christian church, why it happened, and discover how to find truth for themselves.

PO Box 136637
Fort Worth, TX 76163
(817)919-7267
www.fourthangelpublications.com

The Bible records that a man came to Jesus one day asking: "Good Master, what good thing shall I do, that I may have eternal life?" Jesus' immediate response was, "if thou wilt enter into life, keep the commandments" (Matthew 19:16, 17). The answer Jesus gave surprises many today, for it is quite different than many assume He would have given. The standard answers, so popular today, are usually such things as repent, believe, be baptized, confess, etc.; but sadly, seldom does one hear "be obedient to God." When Jesus soon returns there will be many professed Christians who will be surprised to hear Him say, "depart from Me, ye that work iniquity" (Matthew 7:21- 23). Remember, iniquity is sin and "sin is the transgression of the law (1 John 3:4). Therefore, an appropriate paraphrase would be "Depart from Me, ye that reject and transgress My commandments." The relationship between love and obedience is clearly seen in such statements of Jesus as: "If you love me, keep my commandments" (John 14:15). "For this is the love of God, that we keep his commandments" (1 John 5:3). "Howbeit in vain do they worship me, teaching for doctrines the commandments of men. For laying aside the commandment of God, ye hold the tradition of men" (Mark 7:7, 8). It is interesting that the only commandment God prefaced with the word "remember" is the very one the majority of the world has forgotten. When God brings this commandment to one's attention they are usually told by their religious leaders not to concern themselves with it for it is now obsolete. This, however, should not come as a surprise for the word of God warned that there would be "false teachers" who would "bring in damnable heresies" and "many shall follow their pernicious ways" and the "truth shall be evil spoken of" (2 Peter 2:1-2). This has truly taken place today. Discover how in The Forgotten Commandment.

PO Box 136637
Fort Worth, TX 76163
(817)919-7267
www.fourthangelpublications.com

THE FOURTH ANGEL'S
PUBLISHING